LISTENING

BY MARI SCHUH

BLUE OWL
BOOKS

TIPS FOR CAREGIVERS

Social and emotional learning (SEL) helps children connect with their emotions and gain a better understanding of themselves. Mindfulness can support this learning and help them develop a kind and inclusive mentality. By incorporating mindfulness and SEL into early learning, students can establish this mentality early and be better equipped to build strong connections and communities.

BEFORE READING

Talk to the student about listening.

Discuss: What does listening mean to you? How does it feel when someone doesn't listen to you? How can people become better listeners?

AFTER READING

Talk to the student about practicing listening.

Discuss: What does it mean to be a good listener? How will practicing active listening make you a better friend? Who in your life is a good listener? How do you feel when someone takes the time to really listen to you?

SEL GOAL

One way students can become better listeners is through practice. Try having students play a listening game in small groups. One student recites a short story while the other students carefully listen. When the story is over, the students write down what they remember about the story. Who were the characters? What happened to them? Make sure the students take turns listening and reciting.

TABLE OF CONTENTS

CHAPTER 1
What Is Listening? 4

CHAPTER 2
Listening Is Important 8

CHAPTER 3
Being a Good Listener 12

GOALS AND TOOLS
Grow with Goals 22
Mindfulness Exercise 22
Glossary 23
To Learn More 23
Index 24

WHAT IS LISTENING?

Luke had fun at the fair. He wants to tell his brother about it. But his brother is busy gaming.

Luke's brother stops playing and **listens**. He learns about the fun Luke had. By listening, he shows he cares about Luke and Luke's feelings.

Listening is different from hearing. We hear sounds, such as alarms or music. But listening is an action. We have to think to do it. It requires us to **focus**.

When we listen, we are **mindful** and present in the moment. We pay attention to what is being said. We **reflect** on what we have heard.

ACTIVE LISTENING

Being a good listener is often called **active listening**. What does this mean? You pay attention. You look the person speaking in the eye. Your responses show that you are actively listening!

CHAPTER 2

LISTENING IS IMPORTANT

Listening builds healthy **relationships**. Good friends are good listeners. Shannon is moving away. She shares her feelings. When Kristen listens, she shows **empathy**. She tries to understand Shannon's feelings.

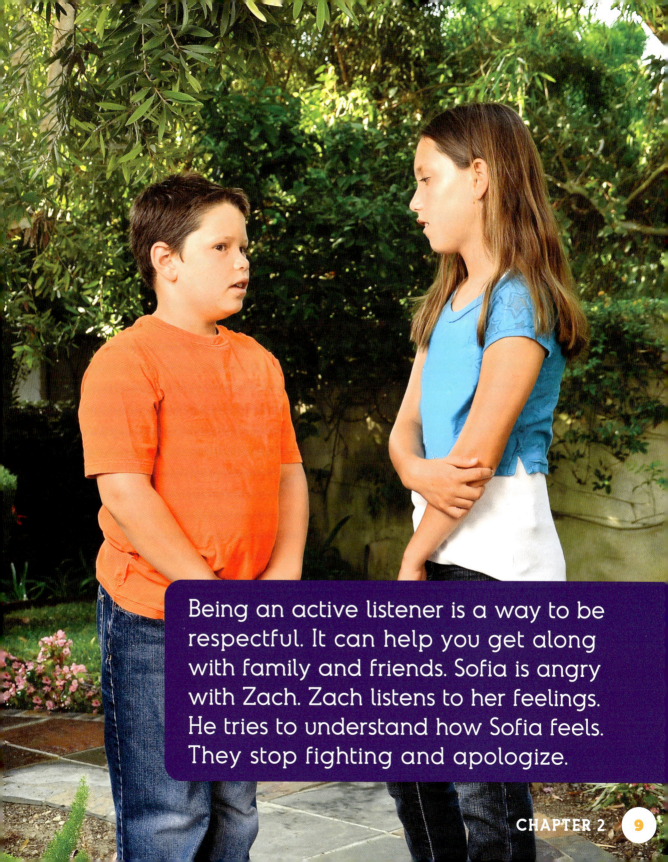

Being an active listener is a way to be respectful. It can help you get along with family and friends. Sofia is angry with Zach. Zach listens to her feelings. He tries to understand how Sofia feels. They stop fighting and apologize.

tutor

Listening is an important part of learning. When you listen, you pay attention and take in information. Juno listens to her tutor explain a math problem. It helps her understand how to solve it. She learns something new!

DID YOU KNOW?

It can be hard to listen when you are tired or hungry. Be sure to get enough sleep. Eat healthy foods. Then you will have energy and **patience** to listen!

BEING A GOOD LISTENER

Being a good listener takes practice and patience. It is something you learn to do. Jack's dad tells him about plans for the weekend. Jack hears him, but he doesn't listen.

Jack's dad politely asks Jack to listen. Jack turns off his tablet. He looks at his dad and pays attention. He listens to what his dad says. The weekend plans are exciting!

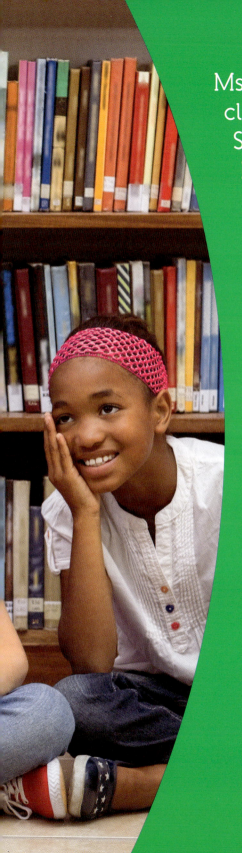

Ms. Marks reads a story to Tova's class. Tova pays attention. How? She faces Ms. Marks so she can hear her. She sits up and looks at her. She tries not to fidget or daydream. Tova enjoys the story!

BODY LANGUAGE

Listen with your whole body. Sit up, face the person who is talking, and avoid crossing your arms. This is open **body language**. It shows others that you are ready to listen.

Everyone has a right to talk and be heard. Being a good listener means not interrupting. It is being open to people's ideas. **Accept** what they say, and try not to judge them. Don't just focus on what you will say in response. Instead, try to feel what they are feeling.

Henry is excited about soccer practice! He talks quickly. Matt doesn't understand what he is saying. He nicely asks Henry to repeat what he said. This shows Henry that Matt cares. How? It shows that he wants to listen. He is willing to take the time to understand what he is saying.

BE PATIENT

Some people might speak slowly or have a **speech impediment**. Be patient! Don't rush or interrupt them. What they are saying is still important.

Listening is an important part of being a good friend and family member. You listen when your friends are happy and excited. You also listen to their problems. In turn, they listen to you.

Being a good listener can help you learn more about others. Relationships are better when we all listen to one another!

GOALS AND TOOLS

GROW WITH GOALS

Listening can be hard! We become good listeners with practice, patience, and mindfulness.

Goal: Ask someone about their day. Did they have a fun day? Listen to them talk about what they did and how they felt. Remember to listen with your whole body. Then people will see that you are truly listening.

Goal: Think about a time someone listened to you. How did it make you feel?

Goal: How can you become a better listener? Write down the ways. Think about these goals the next time someone shares a story or problem with you.

MINDFULNESS EXERCISE

Becoming a better listener takes practice. Play a listening game to practice mindfulness and listening skills.

1. Sit in a line with friends or family members.

2. The first person in line whispers a sentence to the next person in line.

3. Then that person whispers the same sentence to the next person in line.

4. The last person says the sentence out loud to the group. Is that sentence the same one that the first person said? Reflect on how you did. Were you mindful? Did you listen?

5. Move around in the line and try again!

GLOSSARY

accept
To agree that something is correct, satisfactory, or enough.

active listening
Listening that shows that the listener is engaged, often using open body language.

body language
The gestures, movements, and mannerisms by which people communicate with others.

empathy
The ability to understand and be sensitive to the thoughts and feelings of others.

focus
To concentrate on something.

listens
Pays attention to hear and understand something.

mindful
A mentality achieved by focusing on the present moment and calmly recognizing and accepting your feelings, thoughts, and sensations.

patience
The ability to put up with problems or delays without getting angry or upset.

reflect
To think carefully or seriously about something.

relationships
The ways in which people feel about and behave toward one another, or the ways in which two or more people are connected.

speech impediment
A condition that makes it hard to speak, such as a stutter.

TO LEARN MORE

FACT SURFER

Finding more information is as easy as 1, 2, 3.

1. Go to www.factsurfer.com

2. Enter "**listening**" into the search box.

3. Choose your cover to see a list of websites.

INDEX

accept 16

asks 13, 19

body language 15

cares 5, 19

daydream 15

empathy 8

energy 11

feelings 5, 8, 9, 16

fidget 15

focus 6, 16

healthy foods 11

hearing 6, 12, 15, 16

learns 5, 11, 12, 20

look 6, 13, 15

mindful 6

patience 11, 12, 19

practice 12

reflect 6

relationships 8, 20

respectful 9

sleep 11

speech impediment 19

talking 15, 16, 19

understand 8, 9, 11, 19

Blue Owl Books are published by Jump!, 5357 Penn Avenue South, Minneapolis, MN 55419, www.jumplibrary.com

Copyright © 2021 Jump! International copyright reserved in all countries. No part of this book may be reproduced in any form without written permission from the publisher.

Library of Congress Cataloging-in-Publication Data

Names: Schuh, Mari C., 1975– author.
Title: Listening / by Mari Schuh.
Description: Minneapolis: Jump!, Inc., [2021] | Series: Mindful mentality | "Blue Owl Books." | Includes index. | Audience: Ages 7–10.
Identifiers: LCCN 2019058954 (print)
LCCN 2019058955 (ebook)
ISBN 9781645273806 (library binding)
ISBN 9781645273813 (paperback)
ISBN 9781645273820 (ebook)
Subjects: LCSH: Listening—Juvenile literature.
Classification: LCC BF323.L5 S358 2021 (print)
LCC BF323.L5 (ebook) | DDC 153.6/8—dc23
LC record available at https://lccn.loc.gov/2019058954
LC ebook record available at https://lccn.loc.gov/2019058955

Editor: Jenna Gleisner
Designer: Molly Ballanger

Photo Credits: Dmytro Zinkevych/Dreamstime, cover; Maica/iStock, 1; Duplass/Shutterstock, 3; Dragon Images/Shutterstock, 4, 5; kali9/iStock, 6–7; Poike/iStock, 8; Timothy OLeary/Shutterstock, 9; SDI Productions/iStock, 10–11; Sellwell/Shutterstock, 12, 13; Wavebreakmedia/iStock, 14–15; lisafx/iStock, 16–17; LightField Studios/Shutterstock, 18–19; AnnaStills/iStock, 20–21.

Printed in the United States of America at Corporate Graphics in North Mankato, Minnesota.